USBORNE
BOOK OF THE BRAIN
AND HOW IT WORKS

Dr. Betina Ip

(Neuroscientist, University of Oxford)

Illustrated by Mia Nilsson

Edited by Alex Frith
Designed by Melissa Gandhi

Have you ever wondered how your brain works? How does it learn new skills, such as how to ride a bicycle?

I'm getting really good at riding my bike. I don't even have to think about how to do it, I can just *do* it! I wonder how?

This is what your
BRAIN
looks like.

It's so big, it has to be folded up to fit inside your head.

The folded up parts are a little like mountains and valleys.

A HUMAN BRAIN

Your brain is made of two halves, joined by a bridge. This bridge is called the *corpus callosum* — if you want to know.

SPINAL CORD

Your brain is linked to the rest of your body by a long cable called your spinal cord.

It lets your brain tell the rest of your body what to do...

...and it lets your body tell your brain what's going on, too.

But what does my brain actually DO??

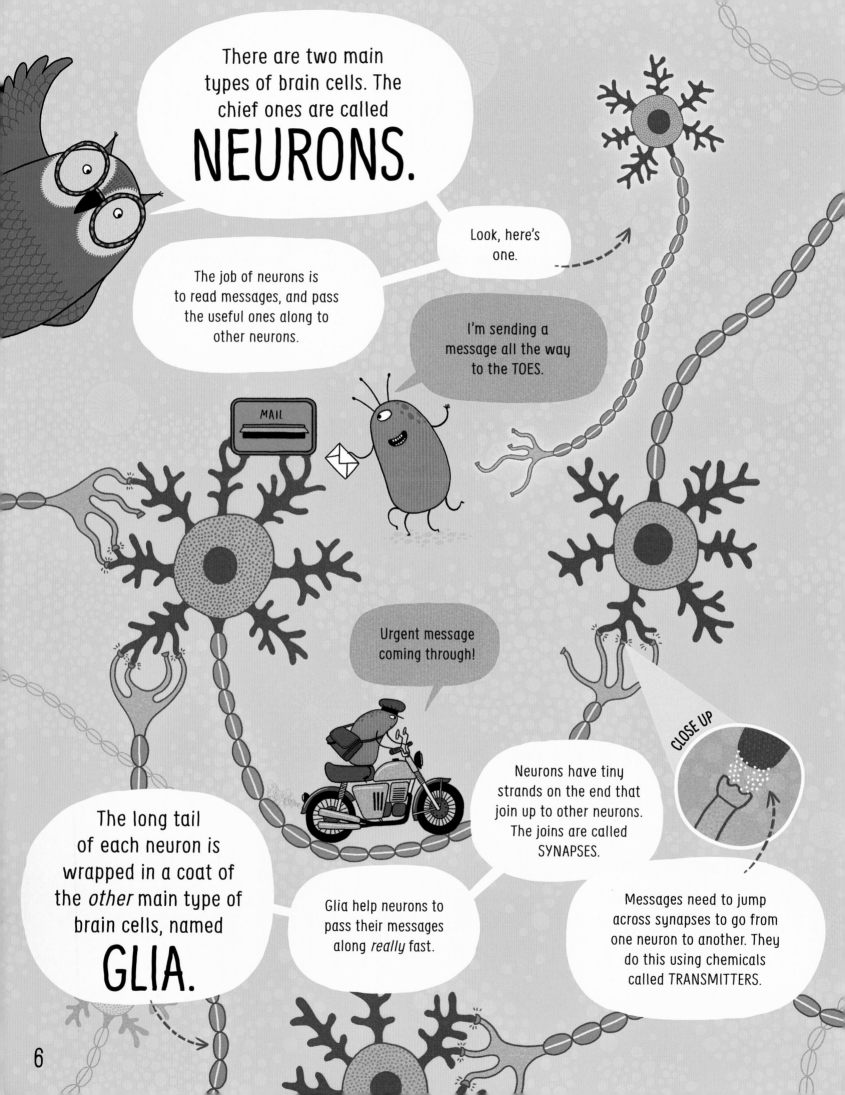

There are two main types of brain cells. The chief ones are called
NEURONS.

The job of neurons is to read messages, and pass the useful ones along to other neurons.

Look, here's one.

I'm sending a message all the way to the TOES.

MAIL

Urgent message coming through!

The long tail of each neuron is wrapped in a coat of the *other* main type of brain cells, named
GLIA.

Glia help neurons to pass their messages along *really* fast.

Neurons have tiny strands on the end that join up to other neurons. The joins are called SYNAPSES.

CLOSE UP

Messages need to jump across synapses to go from one neuron to another. They do this using chemicals called TRANSMITTERS.

6

This message has zoomed along a chain of neurons that runs all down your spinal cord. It's telling your feet to WIGGLE THE TOES.

So every time I use my brain, I'm actually mailing letters?

Yes, in a way!

And it's not just a one-way street. Neurons also carry messages *back* to your brain. For example, they collect messages from your eyes, nose, ears, tongue and skin — your senses.

SENSES AT WORK

I'm touching something sticky!

I can taste something sweet!

Listen! I can hear a wrapper crinkling!

I can smell something good to eat!

Look! A chocolate treat!

I can read all these messages because of ELECTRICITY...

...turn the page to find out how this works.

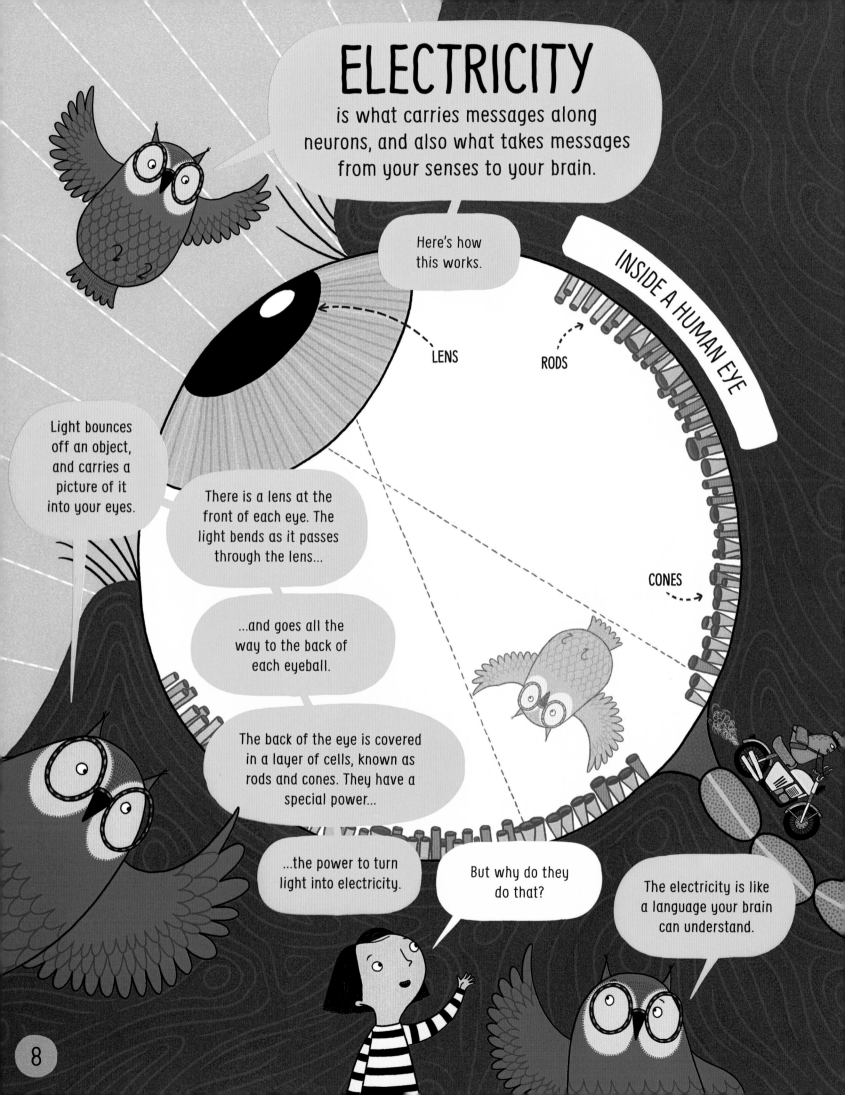

CONES
help see in daytime.

RODS
help see at night.

HOW RODS & CONES WORK

Cone cells can pick out all sorts of details — and colors — in bright daylight.

At night, it's too dark for cones. But rod cells collect information even in dim light.

At the end of each rod and cone, parts called TRANSDUCERS gather all the information...

...and transform it into ELECTRIC MESSAGES that your neurons can understand.

Each message is carried all the way to your brain, where neurons are waiting to read the messages.

Electric message coming through!

Electric message coming through!

Messages travel from your eyes to your brain. Turn the page to find out what happens NEXT.

WHERE IN THE BRAIN?

There's a section of your brain that's like a giant machine designed to DECODE the electric messages.

Messages from your eyes travel to the back of your brain, to a section called the VISUAL CORTEX.

Here, different teams of neurons can understand different types of signals.

Tell me more about SEEING.

MOTION

My team sees things that are moving.

SHAPES

My team sees simple shapes.

LINES

My team picks out straight lines.

MAIL

Electric message coming through!

Speaking of scary things, let's visit the hall of
EMOTIONS.

Emotions help you react to things that go on in the world around you.

When you're very young, your brain learns to recognize emotions in the people around you.

Scientists say there are SIX BASIC EMOTIONS. Each one has its own face.

SURPRISE

ANGER

HAPPINESS

I like the yellow face best! It makes me smile.

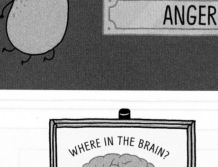

WHERE IN THE BRAIN?

You are here.

That's because your brain likes to copy other people.

When you see someone smiling, it can make *you* smile, and might even make you feel happier.

14

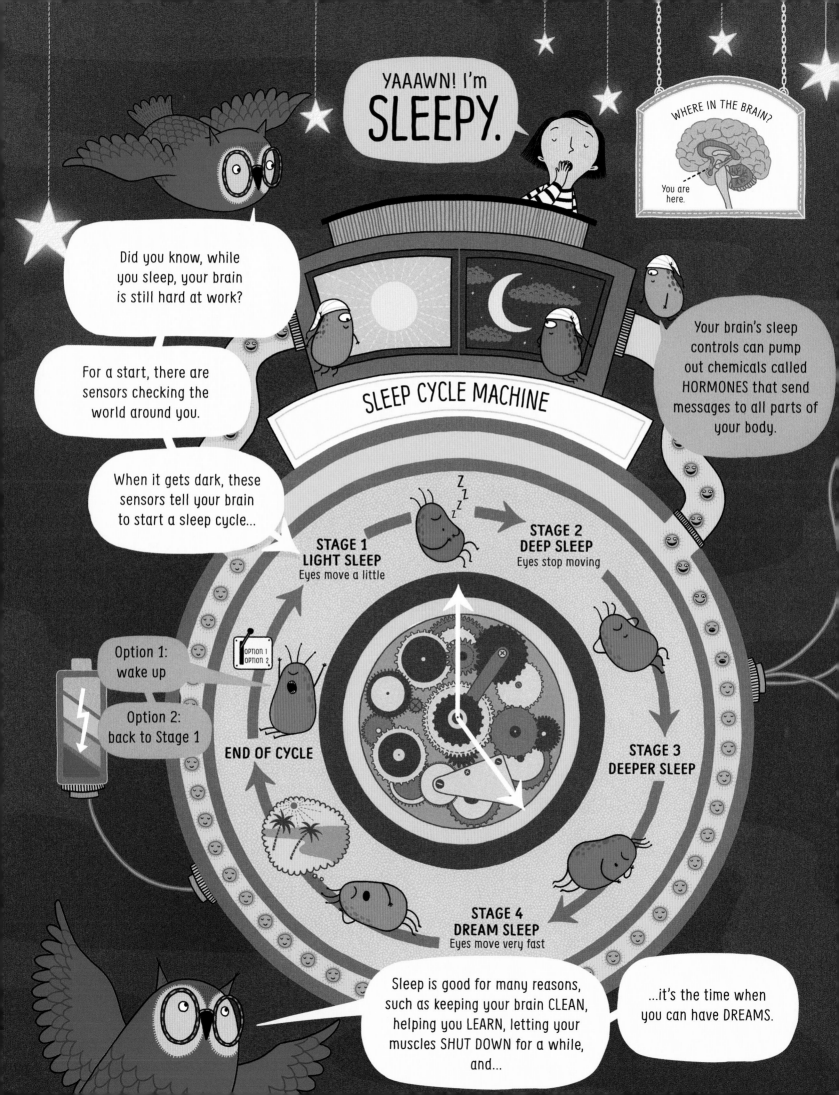

MUSCLE SHUTDOWN

During dream sleep, your brain shuts down connections to your muscles, so you don't act out your dreams.

DREAMING

Dreaming is a big part of being asleep, even if you don't remember your dreams. But no one knows why dreams happen, and if they mean anything.

You only remember a dream if you happen to wake up in the middle of one.

CLEANING

While you sleep, your brain can clean up the spaces between neurons.

LEARNING

Sleeping brains have time to think about all the new things they've discovered that day.

A IS FOR APPLE

French = pomme
Spanish = manzana
Japanese = ringo

RECORDER PRACTICE

Twinkle twinkle little star
= c c g g a a g

Teams of neurons re-play memories while you sleep. This helps you learn.

One of the things your sleeping brain is busy doing is something that happens when you're awake, too. Turn the page to see...

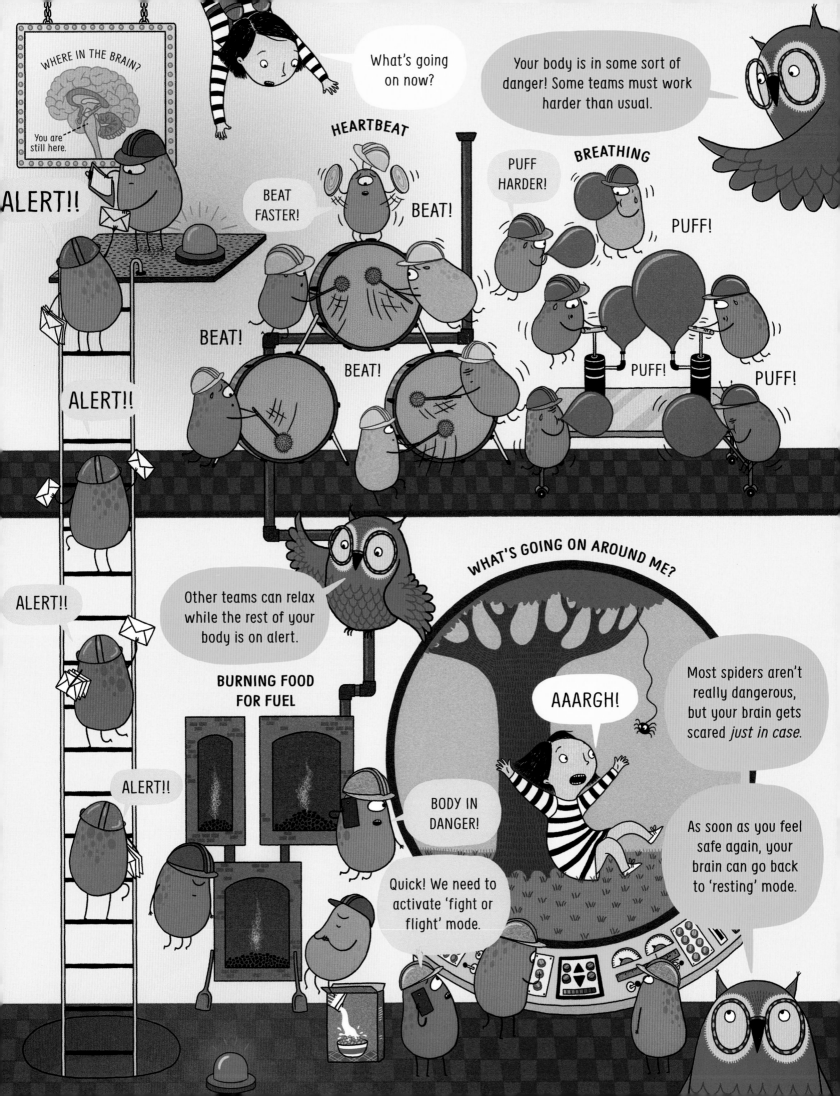

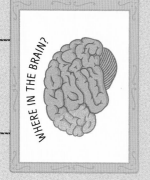

WHERE IN THE BRAIN?

It's time to make a DECISION.
What would you like to do now?

I'm hungry. May I have an ice cream cone, please?

Yes — but which kind of ice cream would you like? You'll have to make a few more decisions...

Most of the things you do need you to make *choices*. Let's imagine each choice is like a thought bubble that you have to pop.

Here's the first bubble. Would you like to go to an ice cream truck...

...or to a café?

A short wait, but not many flavors.

A longer wait, but lots of flavors!

The café — good choice!

NOT TOO EXPENSIVE

On to the next choice. Would you like a single scoop of plain ice cream...

...or three scoops with toppings?

VERY EXPENSIVE

Some neurons can compare how much money you have to spend with how sad you will feel not to have that money any more.

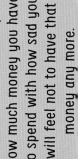

Some of your neurons do the job of deciding how quickly you want this treat.

21

When you use your brain to do anything, you need to send a signal across your tangled branches.

Learning how to do something — whether it's walking, talking or brushing your teeth — is all about finding the best way through.

Practicing a skill is a mixture of two things: *cutting away* branches that you don't need...

...and making the branches you *do* need stronger and stronger.

But it's hard to know which branches to cut away. And that means we all makes lots of mistakes while we're learning.

I'm not afraid of making SOME mistakes if it helps me learn better.

Just like any part of your body, your brain needs

LOOKING AFTER.

Sometimes it's not possible to stop your brain from being unwell, but there are lots of things you can do to help.

Your brain loves EXERCISE! Jumping, dancing, playing — any kind of moving around — makes your brain send messages around your body that make you feel happy.

Your brain loves FOOD! Especially a balanced diet — any mix of foods that keeps your *body* healthy will also keep your *brain* healthy.

Your brain loves OTHER BRAINS! It's good to spend time with your family, your friends, and to meet new people.

Your brain loves SLEEP! It's not just good for learning. Sleep helps you cope with everyday life more easily, and can stop you from feeling too sad.

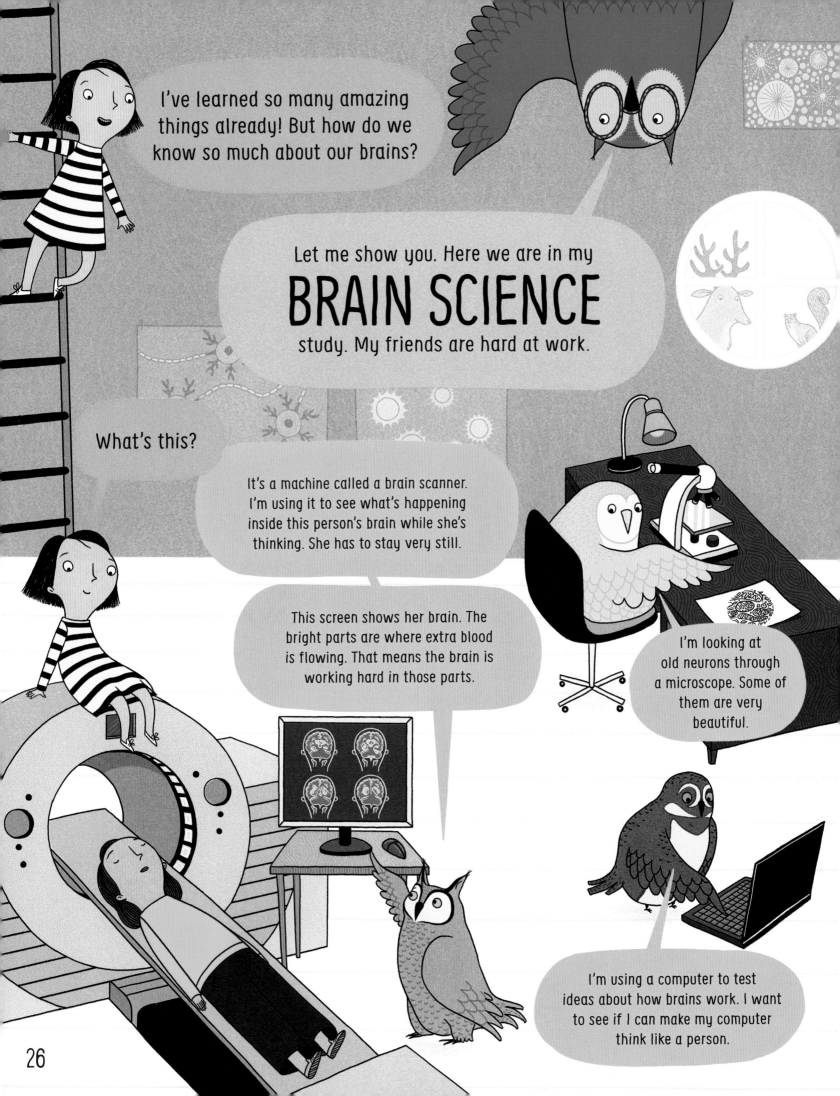

I've learned so many amazing things already! But how do we know so much about our brains?

Let me show you. Here we are in my
BRAIN SCIENCE
study. My friends are hard at work.

What's this?

It's a machine called a brain scanner. I'm using it to see what's happening inside this person's brain while she's thinking. She has to stay very still.

This screen shows her brain. The bright parts are where extra blood is flowing. That means the brain is working hard in those parts.

I'm looking at old neurons through a microscope. Some of them are very beautiful.

I'm using a computer to test ideas about how brains work. I want to see if I can make my computer think like a person.

Here are some
BRAIN FACTS
we *DO* know.

By the time you're
born your brain has
almost all
the neurons it will ever have.

That's why babies
have such big heads.

By the time you're
two years old
your brain has nearly as
many neurons as there are
stars in the galaxy
— around
80 BILLION!

Every time you
think or **remember**
or just ***do*** anything,
you're using millions of neurons
to send messages.

Teenage brains can get
overloaded
with connections between
their neurons.

INDEX

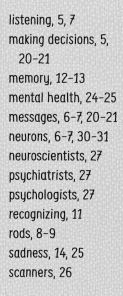

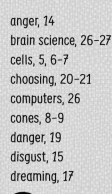

Want to know more about the brain? Visit Usborne Quicklinks
for links to websites with brain facts, videos and activities to try.

Go to usborne.com/Quicklinks and type in the keywords "book of the brain."
Please read the internet safety guidelines at Usborne Quicklinks.
Children should be supervised online.

Brain expert: Professor Holly Bridge,
Nuffield Department of Clinical Neurosciences

US editor: Carrie Armstrong; Managing designer: Stephen Moncrieff

With thanks to Mary Cartwright and Jane Chisholm

Background photograph on p30–31 © Sripfoto/Dreamstime.com

First published in 2020 by Usborne Publishing Ltd.,
Usborne House, 83–85 Saffron Hill, London EC1N 8RT, England.
usborne.com Copyright © 2020 Usborne Publishing Ltd.